Spot On

Spot On

Good Names
for Dogs

Gail Garbutt

First published in Great Britain in 2018 by Spot On.

Cover picture and illustrations by Andrew Walworth.

Edited, designed and produced by Tandem Publishing
http://tandempublishing.yolasite.com/

ISBN: 9978-1-5272-2435-3

10 9 8 7 6 5 4 3 2 1

A CIP catalogue record for this book is available from the British Library.

Printed and bound in Great Britain by CPI Group (UK) Ltd, Croydon CR0 4YY.

CONTENTS

Introduction

Isn't one of life's greatest treats deciding to take on and then pick up a new dog? For those of us that love them, I think it's fair to say that you'll have to name more dogs than children in a lifetime. Choosing a name for a puppy also gives you the chance to have a bit of fun and decide upon a name that puts a smile on your face.

Many of the names in these pages, and all the names of the dogs I've owned, come with two syllables. And not without reason. It must be one of the hardest things to call out an individual dog when it's running in a pack; but this is done all the time by huntsmen with hounds. They believe two syllables are easier for hounds/dogs to tune into and hear.

I have to say that all my dogs had a tendency to be selectively deaf, but perhaps they'd just have been worse had they been called something shorter.

Here's hoping some of these suggestions will prompt you towards a great name for your puppy.

A to Z

Abbey	Anxious
Abbot	Apache
Abysmal	Apathy
Accident	Aptitude
Acrobat	Archer
Admiral	Arctic
Ajax	Armani
Allergy	Atomic
Ambush	Atrocious
Anguish	Attitude
Anthem	Auditor
Anthrax	Aztec
Antic	

Scottish Rivers

Borgie
Naver
Devon
Oykel
Beauly
Foyers
Tummel
Orchy
Lossie
Deveron
Isla
Lochy
Annan
Thurso
Brora
Cassley
Strathy
Garry

A Dog's Sense of Touch

Of the five senses, touch is the one we share most closely with dogs. For most mammals, the first sensation is of being licked by their mother, and through this close bonds are created. Almost all dogs are born into litters of some size, so lying on top of one another or side by side while they suckle make for early sensual experiences.

Puppies and people can forge bonds through touch, similar to those built between a bitch and her puppies. Regular picking up, touching, stroking and cuddling will promote these positive feelings in a puppy, in the long-term making physical contact and grooming easier.

Whiskers with deeply embedded receptor cells at their base are found around the eyes, muzzle and below the jaw on a dog's face. These warn dogs of objects approaching their head, explaining how they're able to run at speed through a thicket without damaging their eyes.

Dogs use touch in five ways: pawing, leaning, mouthing, touching noses and licking. Pawing for attention, leaning to indicate a feeling of insecurity and wanting protection, mouthing to interact with each other, touching noses to find out what the other dog last ate, and licking as a form of affection: dogs like the saltiness of our skin and it provides comfort and pleasure.

Babble	Beaker
Baggage	Beater
Bailiff	Bedlam
Balance	Beetle
Baldrick	Belter
Ballad	Bender
Balthazar	Bingo
Bandage	Biscuit
Bandit	Bisto
Bangle	Blazer
Banish	Blemish
Bantam	Blimey
Banter	Blinis
Bargain	Blizzard
Barnsley	Blunder
Barrel	Blusher
Barrier	Boater
Basher	Bobtail
Battery	Bodice
Battle	Boggle
Bauble	Boisterous
Beacon	Bolter

Bondage	Brummie
Bonkers	Brutus
Bonnie	Bubbly
Bonus	Buckle
Boodle	Buddy
Boosie	Budget
Bouncy	Buffer
Bounder	Buffy
Bowler	Bugle
Braces	Bullion
Bracken	Bumble
Bracket	Bumper
Bradley	Bungi
Bramble	Burma
Bravo	Bursar
Brazen	Busby
Bridle	Buster
Brindle	Butler
Bristol	Buttie
Britches	Buttons
Broker	Buttress
Bruiser	Buxom

When God had made the earth and sky,
The flowers and the trees,
He then made all the animals,
The fish, the birds and bees.

And when at last he'd finished,
Not one was quite the same
He said "I'll walk this world of mine
And give each one a name."

And so he travelled far and wide,
And everywhere he went,
A little creature followed him,
Until its strength was spent.

When all were named upon the earth,
And in the sky and sea,
The little creature said "Dear Lord,
There's not one left for me"

Kindly the Father said to him,
"I've left you to the end.
I've turned my own name back to front,
And called you DOG, my friend."

Anon

Cable	Casket
Cactus	Cassock
Caddie	Casual
Cadger	Caustic
Caesar	Caution
Calico	Cautious
Camphor	Cavity
Candid	Cedric
Cannibal	Celtic
Cannon	Censor
Canopy	Census
Caper	Chairman
Capsule	Champion
Captain	Chaos
Capture	Chappie
Carnage	Chapter
Carnival	Charcoal
Cartoon	Charmer
Cartridge	Chastity

Chatterbox	Cocktail
Chaucer	Codger
Cherub	Colic
Chieftain	Colonel
Chipper	Coma
Chronic	Combat
Chuckle	Comedy
Chukka	Comet
Chunky	Comfort
Chutney	Comic
Citric	Comma
Claret	Compact
Classic	Complex
Climax	Compost
Clinker	Compound
Clutter	Comrade
Cobbler	Concord

Condor

Conflict

Conker

Convict

Corky

Corporal

Corset

Costa

Cracker

Crackle

Crafty

Crasher

Crazy

Cribbage

Crikey

Crinkle

Crisis

Crotchet

Cruiser

Crumble

Crumpet

Crunchy

Crusty

Crutches

Cryptic

Cubit

Cuddles

Culprit

Culture

Cunning

Curious

Curley

Curtsey

The Games People Play

A great choice here, whether it's something you play as a family, a sport you excel at or how you spend an afternoon at the beach. I've only listed a few, and without doubt my favourite game is Freda.

- Ludo • Scrabble • Trumps •
- Cribbage • Rummy • Polo •
- Chukka • Rugger • Rugby •
- Frisbee • Cluedo • Cricket •
- Hopscotch • Chequers •
- Poker • Uno • Snooker •
- Freda •

The dog is a gentleman;
I hope to go to his heaven, not man's.
Mark Twain

He is your friend, your partner, your
defender, your dog. You are his life, his love,
his leader. He will be yours, faithful and
true, to the last beat of his heart. You owe it
to him to be worthy of such devotion.
Anon

Dabble	Digger	Dopey
Dainty	Digit	Double
Damage	Dimple	Doubter
Damper	Dior	Dowry
Dapple	Diploma	Draggle
Dasher	Dipper	Drastic
Dawdle	Dippy	Dribble
Dazzle	Dither	Drivel
Dealer	Ditto	Drizzle
Decibel	Diva	Drowsy
Deluge	Dividend	Druid
Demon	Dizzy	Drummer
Destiny	Dodger	Dubious
Devious	Dollar	Dumpy
Dexter	Dollop	Dwindle
Dialect	Dolly	Dylan
Dibber	Domino	Dynamic
Diesel	Doodle	Dynamite

A Dog's Sense of Taste

We're the winners here, with 9,000 taste buds compared to a dog's 1,706 – a large disparity. Dogs' taste buds are situated at the tip of their tongues, providing the same information as ours: bitter, sweet, sour and salt.

In the wild, ancestors of the modern domesticated dog would have lived off an 80 per cent meat diet. Water would have been a priority, given that meat is particularly salty, and so their taste buds evolved to be sophisticated enough to taste water.

Being omnivores, they would also have eaten fruit and vegetables in the wild, which would have developed their liking for sweet flavours. But we all know they'll eat almost anything! Their highly sophisticated sense of smell comes into play: if it smells good, they believe it's going to taste good too.

NAMING BY TYPE

This idea comes from my grandmother who couldn't think of a name for her puppy. Still without a name after a fortnight she resorted to calling him his breed – Boxer.

It works for some others too:

- Basset
- Beagle
- Border
- Boxer
- Clumber
- Collie
- Lucas
- Lurcher
- Mastiff
- Mongrel
- Pointer
- Poodle
- Scottie
- Springer
- Watch Dog
- Whippet

Eager

Earnest

Ebony

Echo

Ecstasy

Ecstatic

Editor

Ember

Emblem

Embroil

Empty

Energy

Ensign

Entity

Envoy

Equity

Ethnic

Ethos

Eureka

Everest

Excess

Exotic

Extra

Faggot	Fetish
Fagin	Fettle
Failure	Feudal
Falstaff	Fever
Famish	Fickle
Famous	Fiddle
Fantasy	Fiddler
Fateful	Fidget
Fathom	Fiery
Favour	Fifi
Fearless	Filthy
Fearsome	Firework
Feisty	Fixture
Fender	Fizzer
Ferment	Fizzle
Fester	Flagon
Festival	Flasher
Festive	Flaxen

Flippant	Frantic
Flirt	Frazzle
Flirty	Freckle
Floosie	Frenzy
Flounder	Fresco
Flourish	Friction
Flunky	Frisbee
Flurry	Frisky
Fluster	Frivolous
Flutter	Frolic
Foible	Frostie
Fondle	Frugal
Foolish	Frumpy
Forfeit	Fuddle
Fortress	Fungus
Fortune	Fussy
Fosters	

The Ages of Man

I first came across this idea when a friend gave her husband a Border puppy called 'Forty'. The idea works for most decades:

Twenty

Thirty

Forty

Fifty

Sixty...

... you get the drift...

Gamble	Grappa
Garland	Grapple
Garnish	Gravy
Gaudy	Greedy
General	Griddle
Genuine	Griffin
Giddy	Grinner
Giggle	Gripper
Ginger	Grizzly
Glamour	Gromit
Glimmer	Groper
Glitter	Grotto
Goblet	Growler
Google	Grumpy
Gossip	Gucci
Governor	Guinness
Grammar	Gunner
Graphic	Gypsy

Themes from Favourite Authors

One set of cousins always uses names from Dickens' novels:

- Peggotty • Dorrit •
- Micawber • Pip • Dombey •
- Fagin • Tuggs • Wosky •
- Tibbs • Tozer • Tupple •
- Toodle • Traddles •
- Skiffins • Sparkins •
- Swiveller • Slowboy •
- Slunkey • Snubbin •
- Drummle • Pipkin •
- Littimer •

Hamper

Handful

Handsome

Harpic

Hassle

Havoc

Hazard

Hectic

Herald

Hermes

Hermit

Hero

Hippo

Hippy

Hipster

Homer

Honey

Hopeless

Hostile

Hearing in Dogs

We all know a dog's sense of hearing is much keener than ours. The canine sense of hearing is second only to their sense of smell. There isn't a great difference between breeds, but those with prick ears and manoeuvrable ears benefit from marginally better hearing.

Dogs can pick up sounds from four times the distance that we're able to – great for guarding the house, and, compared to us, they hear almost double the range of frequencies. Canines have the ability for each ear to hear separately, so they can hear you talking on one side and birdsong on the other. So this explains their sleeping through the sounds of the TV but waking up with the slightest rustle of the treat packet.

Their lives are dominated by sounds and smells, which continues to be of benefit to us in so many ways. Searching for lost walkers in the mountains, and after earthquakes and avalanches; tracking people from crime scenes and helping the police look for drugs in vehicles – the list goes on...

As dogs age, rather like my husband, their sense of hearing decreases.

LITERARY LEGENDS

We all have our favourites, the problem being that if you have a puppy one's never quite sure how he or she will turn out. With the benefit of hindsight I can see that our Patterdale cross would have made a great 'Gnasher'.

Lassie • Drummond • Snoopy
• Toto • Snowy • Cerberus
• Perdida • Dipstick •
Gnasher • Fluffy • Timothy •
Ponto • Diogenes • Gusty
• Rover • Argus
• Bull's Eye •
Jock • Tartar • Zebedee
• Montmorency •
Skeet • Buck • Breakspear

Idiom

Imperial

Impish

Impulse

Incident

Income

Index

Indigo

Inkling

Inky

Insult

Interest

Irksome

A Dog's Sight

Being descendants of wolves, dogs have eyes that developed for hunting at night, sensitive to low light levels and with good motion sensors, which explains to me why so many dogs are happy chasing a ball. Our vision is different, as we've become diurnal creatures, with a higher sense of colour spectrums and greater detailed vision.

Dogs can see some colour: their spectrum lies between yellow and blue, while ours is blue, green and red. Notice how in agility classes the objects tend to be painted blue and yellow.

We're known to have 20:20 vision (well, the lucky ones among us do) whilst dogs have 20:80 vision: we can see clearly four times further than they can.

Predator species, including us and dogs, tend to have eyes set at the front of the head, whereas prey species (such as horses) have their eyes set further back towards the side of their heads, to give them a greater field of vision to see their predators. How well a dog perceives depth will be due in part to where their eyes are set; dogs with eyes closer together will have a vision overlap, which provides binocular vision. This is important for tricks such as jumping and catching, skills used by all predators.

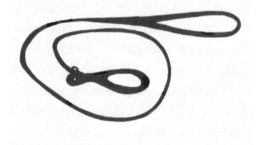

Money Matters

Many of these names will be lost on anyone under thirty, but they still make a good theme.

- Dime • Dinar • Dollar •
Drachma • Ducat • Farthing
- Florin • Guilder • Guinea
- Kopeck • Krona • Lira •
- Lolly • Nickel • Pfennig •
Rouble • Rupee • Shekel •
- Shilling • Sixpence •
Sovereign • Tuppence • Zloty •

Jaunty

Java

Jerkin

Jeroboam

Jester

Jingle

Jockey

Joker

Jollity

Jostle

Journal

Jovial

Jubilant

Jumble

Junior

Junket

DOGS WITH FAMOUS OWNERS

Buddy   Bill Clinton when President of the USA.

Susie   Queen Elizabeth II, her first Corgi.

Diamond   Sir Isaac Newton. Said to be his favourite dog; Diamond once knocked over a candle, burning manuscripts containing Newton's notes on twenty years of experiments.

Buster   Sir Roy Hattersley.

Boatswain   Lord Byron. This was his black and white Newfoundland, whose tomb is larger than the one erected for Byron himself.

Flush   Elizabeth Barrett Browning.

Rufus & **Dodo**   Sir Winston Churchill.

Looty   Queen Victoria. A devoted animal-lover, the Queen's royal patronage added the 'R' to the SPCA in 1840. Looty, a Pekingese from China, was given to her by Captain Hart Dunne of the 99th Regiment during the Second Opium War.

Boye   Prince Rupert of the Rhine. During the Civil War, as the Royalist commander, Prince Rupert of the Rhine had an adored white hunting poodle called Boye; he was trained to cock his leg and pee whenever the name of Pym, the Parliamentarian commander, was mentioned.

Kaiser

Keeper

Kermit

Kestrel

Kindle

Kinky

Kipling

Kipper

Knacker

Knocker

Knockers

Kudos

Kummel

MILITARY MATTERS

A long with the majority of my friends I've scrubbed and moved from Army quarter to Army quarter, and not always with good grace. These choices came while thinking of those still having to iron a khaki shirt.

Ambush

Apache

Armour

Bomber

Bugle

Busby

Captain

Colonel

Combat

Comrade

Corporal

General

Guardsman

Gunner

Hussar

Khaki

Lancer

Major

Medic

Musket

Officer

Pistol

Platoon

Rifle

Sapper

Sergeant

Soldier

Squadron

Status

Trooper

Trumpet

Warrior

Weapon

Lawless

Ledger

Legacy

Legend

Lethal

Limit

Loaded

Loafer

Lodger

Logic

Loony

Loopy

Lucky

Lumber

Lurgy

Lyric

Macho	Meddler
Madness	Melchid
Magic	Melody
Magnet	Menace
Magnum	Mentor
Maiden	Merchant
Mangle	Meteor
Manic	Methuselah
Martini	Midge
Master	Midget
Matrix	Miessen
Maxim	Mighty
Mayhem	Millet
Meadow	Minster

Minus	Mortal
Missile	Mortar
Mission	Motley
Misty	Muddle
Mittens	Muffle
Mobile	Mumble
Moët	Murmur
Mogul	Music
Mohawk	Musket
Molasses	Mustard
Monitor	Musty
Monkey	Mystic
Monstrous	Mystro

Dirty Dogs

Aren't they the worst, and how we all dread going to see friends whose awful dog 'rogers' your leg – you don't forget them though!

- Ardent • Rampant •
Climax • Roger • Bollocks •
Chopper • Playboy • Dodgy
• Fetish • Bounder • Trousers
• Randy • Lusty • Alfie •
• Whopper •

Naughty

Nawab

Nectar

Needy

Nibbler

Nibbles

Nickle

Nimble

Nipper

Nonsense

Normal

Nugget

Nuisance

Numptee

Nutmeg

Couples

I've never been brave enough to take on two puppies at the same time. However, some do, and here are a few thoughts. Or you can choose one name and then wait until a second dog comes along later to use the other part.

Custom & Excise
Bobby & Dazzler
Bangers & Mash
Boots & Britches
Bubble & Squeak
Artful & Dodger
Asterix & Obelix
Anglo & Saxon
Bib & Tucker
Crumpet & Muffin
Biceps & Triceps
Pestle & Mortar
Noughts & Crosses
Gilbert & Sullivan
Holmes & Watson

Iliad & Odyssey
Double & Trouble
Flotsam & Jetsam
Creepy & Crawly
Brandy & Ginger
Sticky & Wicket
Crotchet & Quaver
Jeeves & Wooster
Frodo & Bilbo
Jimmy & Riddle
Bilbo & Baggins
Harris & Lewis
Chitter & Chatter
Romulus & Remus
Tom & Foolery
Topsy & Turvey
Neeps & Tatties
Rack & Ruin
Rough & Tumble
Pitter & Patter
Ranter & Raver
Fuss & Bother
Hunky & Dory
Butch & Spike
Homer & Marge
Chapter & Verse

Oddity

Odious

Odour

Offal

Officer

Okra

Omega

Omen

Onerous

Optic

Option

Oracle

Orbit

Orchard

Orgy

Orkney

Outlaw

Overtime

Overture

The Bridge Set

If like me you came to bridge later in life then you have probably left it too late to use this as a theme to name all your dogs. Still, some of these names are good enough just to pick out on their own account.

Stayman

Chicago

Rubber

Shuffle

Trick

Trumps

Ruffing

Honour

Singleton

Doubleton

Slam

Dummy

Duplicate

Discard

Blackwood

Declarer

Auction

Bidding

Finesse

Signal

Minor

Major

Penalty

Dealer

Contract

Packet	Permit
Paddle	Perry
Paddock	Piccolo
Padre	Pickle
Pagan	Picnic
Pageant	Pilot
Pancake	Piper
Paradise	Pistol
Partner	Piston
Pauper	Pixie
Peddler	Planet
Pelmet	Plato
Penalty	Playboy
Perfect	Playful
Perjury	Plover

Plummet	Problem
Plunder	Profit
Pluto	Progress
Polar	Protest
Polo	Proverb
Pommel	Prowler
Popper	Prozac
Porsche	Publican
Portion	Pudding
Posy	Puffin
Prattle	Pukka
Premium	Purdey
Present	Purpose
Preston	Puzzle
Prickle	

For Golfers

Tempo
Caddie
Handicap
Sclaff
Topping
Putter
Troon
Fairway
Driver
Bandit
Buggy
Bunker
Hacker
Clubhouse
Gimmies
Eagle
Birdie
Divots
Bogey

Quarrel
Quaver
Query
Question
Quibble
Quiver

Breweries

Marston
Fullers
Weston (cider)
Badger
Guinness
Boddie (for Boddington)
Belhaven
Brakspear
Brewer
Butcombe
Carling
Tetley
Fosters
Wadworth
Naylor
Otley
Otter
Blackthorn
Jennings
Meantime
Theakston
Wychwood
Ilkley

Rabble	Ratio	Rivet
Racer	Rattle	Rocker
Racket	Ratty	Rocket
Radar	Raucous	Rolex
Radical	Razzle	Roller
Radium	Rebel	Rommel
Radius	Reflex	Romper
Radley	Refuge	Rouble
Raffle	Regent	Roulade
Ragged	Relic	Rover
Raider	Relish	Rowdy
Rambler	Rehab	Rubble
Rampant	Remedy	Rudolph
Random	Rhyme	Ruffian
Randy	Rhythm	Ruffle
Ranger	Riddle	Rumble
Ransom	Riffle	Rumour
Rascal	Ripper	Rumple
Ratchet	Ripple	Rumpus
Ratify	Ritzy	Rusty

For Geeks

Gizmo

Gadget

Widget

Google

Blogger

Fitter

Twitter

Sabre	Scrummage	Sizzle
Safari	Scrumpy	Skipper
Sailor	Scrunchie	Skirmish
Saladin	Scruple	Slammer
Salvage	Senior	Slander
Sambo	Sentry	Sligo
Sanction	Sergeant	Slipper
Sanity	Settler	Slobber
Santos	Shabby	Smartie
Saucy	Shaker	Smasher
Savage	Shamble	Smitten
Scamper	Shandy	Smoothie
Scampi	Shanty	Smudge
Scandal	Sheriff	Smuggle
Scoffer	Shifty	Smuggler
Scooby	Shuffle	Smutty
Scoundrel	Siesta	Snipe
Scramble	Silage	Snooty
Scribble	Simnel	Soda

Solar	Sprinter	Stroppy
Soldier	Sprocket	Struggle
Sonar	Squabble	Stubble
Spangle	Squatter	Stubby
Sparkle	Squeamish	Stumpy
Sparky	Squiffy	Sturdy
Spartan	Stadium	Suitor
Specify	Static	Suleiman
Speckle	Status	Sultan
Speedy	Steamer	Sunny
Splatter	Stigma	Suspect
Splodge	Stoic	Swagger
Splutter	Straggler	Swarthy
Spoiler	Strategy	Sweeper
Spoof	Stretcher	Sweepy
Spooky	Striker	Swindle
Sporran	Stripper	Swinger
Sprinkle	Stroller	Swivel

FOODIES

So often used as it's a great theme, too many to list them all.

Pudding

Treacle

Honey

Gravy

Ketchup

Crumble

Relish

Pesto

Chutney

Pickle

Crumpet & Muffin

Flapjack

Gristle

Blinis	Fritter
Noodle	Pretzel
Strudel	Radish
Brownie	Raisin
Lobster	Peanut
Smartie	Cobble
Coco	Coffee
Bendicks	Cracker
Stilton	Crouton
Cookie	Muffin
Bounty	Nugget
Nutmeg	Okra
Crunchie	Pickles
Cumin	Medlar
Ginger	Waffle
Pepper	Dumpling
Pumpkin	Bisto
Bagel	Truffle
Biscuit	Mocha
Fudge	Mango

Tablet	Tarnish	Thimble
Tabloid	Tartan	Thistle
Tactic	Tassel	Thrasher
Taffeta	Tatler	Thunder
Taffie	Tatters	Ticket
Taffy	Tattle	Tickle
Tailor	Tattoo	Tickle
Talent	Tawny	Tiffany
Tally	Teasel	Tiffin
Tamper	Teaser	Tilly
Tandem	Teddy	Tinker
Tangent	Temper	Tintin
Tangle	Terrific	Tipple
Tango	Tetley	Tipster
Tankard	Texture	Tipsy
Tantrum	Therapy	Titus
Tardy	Thesis	Toasted

Toaster	Trespass	Truckle
Toffee	Tribute	Truffle
Tonic	Trickle	Trumper
Topic	Tricky	Trumps
Topper	Triden	Tuffy
Topsy	Trident	Tumble
Towzer	Trigger	Tumbler
Toxic	Trinket	Tunic
Traction	Triple	Tuppence
Trader	Triton	Turban
Traffic	Triumph	Turbo
Treacle	Trixie	Turbot
Treasure	Trooper	Turpin
Trellis	Trophy	Tweedie
Tremble	Trottle	Twinkle
Tremor	Trousers	Twister

CRICKET

Of course it doesn't just have to be cricket – there's rugby, football, hockey, darts, snooker or netball.

Lobster

Blowers

Over

Spins

Asterisk

Batsman

Ashes

Striker

Bouncer

Opener

Floater

Howzat

Chucker

Bouncer

Zooter

Trundle

Trimmer

Innings

Wicket

Swerver

Nibble

Maiden

Fieldsman

Jaffa

Bowler

Stumper

Uniform

Uppish

Uproar

Upset

Upstart

Urchin

Urgent

Useful

Useless

Usher

Utter

SHIPPING STATIONS

For anyone who loves messing about on boats.

Fastnet

Fitzroy

Dover

Biscay

Bailey

Rockall

Malin

Humber

Dogger

Viking

Forties

Fisher

Vagrant	Vermin
Valour	Vermouth
Value	Vertigo
Vampire	Vespers
Vandal	Vessel
Vanish	Vestry
Varsity	Veteran
Varsity	Victor
Vatican	Victory
Velocity	Viking
Velvet	Villain
Veneer	Vintage
Venture	Virago
Venus	Virtue
Verger	Voodoo

DRINKING FRIENDS

Brandy & Ginger
Whisky & Soda
Claret
Flagon
Guinness
Bender
Blotto
Bubbly
Rose
Bottle
Stout
Tipple
Tonic
Pepsi & Cola
Grappa
Bombay & Sapphire
Bacardi
Dram
Boozer

A Dog's Amazing Sense of Smell

All dogs love sniffing everything, and here's why – they see their world through smells.

A dog's nose and system for processing what they smell is extraordinarily sophisticated. The scent-detecting cells in human noses collectively amount to the size of a postage stamp; in a dog's, the area nearly covers the size of a piece of A4 paper. And the part of a dog's brain devoted to processing smells is understood to be forty times larger than ours. We have five million scent receptors, whilst the number in dogs varies from breed to breed: a Bloodhound has 300 million.

We have used their amazing sense of smell to our advantage: dogs are able to seek out drugs and explosives, and in medicine some dogs show the ability to smell out human cancers. Not only do dogs smell the here and now, they can translate, through smell, the passage of time and emotions.

Between dogs this sense of smell is a crucial form of communication. All dogs, both wild and domestic, leave their urine splashed on almost every passing object to give out messages about themselves. This is then picked up by the next passing dog, who is able to detect and translate the information left, not only by the last peeing dog but the others who came before.

Wager	Whistle
Wallop	Whistler
Warrior	Whopper
Warwick	Wicket
Waster	Widgeon
Watchman	Widget
Wattage	Willow
Wealthy	Winkle
Weapon	Winner
Weasel	Witter
Webster	Wobble
Welcome	Wonky
Whatnot	Worry
Wheaten	Wotchit
Wheedle	Wotnot
Whisker	Wrangle
Whiskers	Wrestler
Whisky	Wriggle
Whisper	Wrinkle

The Smart Set

Having been brought up with scruffy terriers, I couldn't really consider any of these names for my own dogs. But thinking of elegant Greyhounds, Great Danes and Whippets, well they'd certainly be able to carry off some of these.

- Archer • Countess •
- Dowager • Duchy •
- Duke & Duchess • Eminence
- Emperor • Empire • Empress
- Kaiser • Marquis • Mogul
- Monarch • Palace • Peerage
- Rani • Regal •
- Rex & Regina • Viceroy •

Yankee

Yarrow

Yeoman

Yokel

Yucca

Zealot

Zero

Zigzag

Zipper

Zodiac

Zombie

Zulu

Zuzu

Rich Bitches

Boujis	Ivana
Prada	Melania
Diva	Prada
Dior	Ruby
Rehab	Emerald
Fifi	Gucci
Fetish	Prima & Donna
Knockers	Sassie
Bodice	Tatler
Sapphire	Harpers
Floosie	Corset
Ritzy	Diamond
Fluffy	Chelsea
Monaco	

With eye upraised his master's looks to scan,
The joy, the solace, and the aid of man;
The rich man's guardian and the poor man's
    friend
The only creature faithful to the end.

George Crabbe

And at the end...

Four-Feet

I have done mostly what most men do,
And pushed it out of my mind;
But I can't forget, if I wanted to,
Four-Feet trotting behind.

Day after day, the whole day through—
Wherever my road inclined—
Four-Feet said, "I am coming with you!"
And trotted along behind.

Now I must go by some other round,—
Which I shall never find—
Somewhere that does not carry the sound
Of Four-Feet trotting behind.

Rudyard Kipling

ACKNOWLEDGEMENTS

Thanks to Celia, Ally, Bertie, Rollo and Garbo
who've all helped get this on the road.

About the Author

Gail was bought up with a series of different breeds of dogs in a freezing house in Gloucestershire. One way or another they always seemed to come first; after all, they had their beds in front of the Aga!

Once married, Gail bought her first terrier, Floosie, and has since owned Ditto, Rubble and now Sixty. She lives in Wiltshire with her husband and has two grown-up sons.